Don't Reply All

18 Email Tactics That Help You Write Better Emails and Improve Communication with Your Team

By

Hassan Osman

Don't Reply All: 18 Email Tactics That Help You Write Better Emails and Improve Communication with Your Team
Copyright © 2015 by Hassan Osman.

Liability Disclaimer and FTC Notice

The purpose of this book is to provide the user with general information about the subject matter presented. This book is for entertainment purposes only. This book is not intended, nor should the user consider it, to be legal advice for a specific situation. The author, company, and publisher make no representations or warranties with respect to the accuracy, fitness, completeness, or applicability of the contents of this book. They disclaim any merchantability, fitness or warranties, whether expressed or implied. The author, company, and publisher shall in no event be held liable for any loss or other damages, including but not limited to special, incidental, consequential, or other damages. This disclaimer applies to any damages by any failure of performance, error, omission, interruption, deletion, defect, delay in operation or transmission, computer malware, communication line failure, theft or destruction or unauthorized access to, or use of record, whether for breach of contract, tort, negligence, or under any other cause of action.

By reading this book, you agree that the use of it is entirely at your own risk and that you are solely responsible for your use of the contents. The advice of a competent legal counsel (or any other professional) should be sought. The author, company, and publisher do not warrant the performance, effectiveness or applicability of any sites or references listed in this book. Some links are affiliate links. This means that if you decide to make a purchase after clicking on some links, the author will make a commission. All references and links are for information purposes only and are not warranted for content, accuracy or any other implied or explicit purpose.

Table of Contents

Introduction

Here's an email from John:

Subject: Blah blah blah

Team,

Blah blah blah, blah blah blah blah blah. Blah blah blah blah blah blah blah blah blah. Blah blah blah blah blah blah; blah blah blah blah blah. Blah, blah blah, blah blah blah - blah blah. Blah blah blah blah blah, blah blah blah blah blah. Blah blah blah blah blah blah? Blah blah blah blah blah blah blah blah blah.

Blah blah blah blah blah blah blah blah. Blah blah blah blah blah blah blah blah blah. Blah blah blah blah blah blah; blah blah blah blah blah. Blah blah, blah blah, blah blah - blah blah. Oh, and by the way, I need this urgently before the end of day tomorrow. Blah blah blah blah blah, blah blah blah blah blah. Blah blah blah blah blah blah. Blah blah blah blah blah blah blah blah blah? Blah blah blah blah.

Blah blah blah blah blah blah blah blah. Blah blah blah blah blah blah blah blah. Blah blah blah blah blah blah; blah blah blah blah blah? Blah blah, blah blah, blah blah - blah blah. Blah blah blah blah blah, blah blah blah blah blah? Blah blah blah blah blah blah. Blah blah blah blah blah blah blah blah.

Thoughts?

John

John's email *sucks*.

Here are four reasons why.

Reason 1: Too long

First, it's too long.

Reading a message doesn't just take time; it takes time *and* mental energy.

As the unlucky recipient of this email, I need to read it, process it, analyze it, and then decide what to do with it.

John has sent me a load of jargon-laden nonsense, and by doing so, he put the onus on *me* to determine what information is relevant and what is not. That's never fun.

We'll discuss how to properly break long emails down in tactic 4.

Reason 2: Hidden actions and questions

Second, the action items and questions that John wants the team to follow up on are hidden in a forest of nonsense.

There are three question marks in three separate paragraphs. I'm not sure who those are directed at.

I also see what *seems* to be an action item without a clear owner, description, or deadline.

Moreover, John barely hinted at the fact that he needs "this urgently before the end of day tomorrow" right in the middle of the second paragraph.

If I had scanned the email the first time I read it—which is how I usually read emails these days—I would not have picked up on that, and his urgent request would have been missed. (By the way, the "need this urgently" phrase really is included in the example above. If you missed it too, that just reinforces my point.)

We'll address the hidden actions and questions problem in tactics 1 and 5.

Reason 3: Useless subject line

The subject line is meaningless.

John didn't summarize what he wanted, didn't give any indication that the email included actions, and didn't give a directive that one of his requests is urgent.

A subject line needs to explain what the email is about before I open it. Writing anything else decreases the chances that it'll be read and just adds confusion.

Tactic 2 will show you how to write the perfect subject line.

Reason 4: Ends with an open-ended question

Ending an email with "Thoughts?" is a problem for a couple of reasons.

First, it invites the team to reply all and share their random ideas about what they think, which adds more emails and confusion to the mix.

Second, it's a passive, open-ended question that doesn't guide the recipient to answer in a specific way, which could introduce more questions in the process and possibly even mask the original intent of the email.

Open questions are generally better suited to be discussed in a meeting instead.

We'll cover how to ask open-ended questions the right way in tactic 9.

Why I Wrote This Book

I get over 400 emails a day.

And I'm not even that special or popular.

I'm just a manager who interacts with multiple teams spread across the world.

I deal with emails from my team members, my management chain, my clients, and my peers on a daily basis.

So I wrote this book out of frustration.

My frustration is not with the *quantity* of emails that I get, but rather with the *quality* of emails.

In other words, it's not that I get a lot of emails. It's that I get a lot of *bad* emails.

And those bad emails consequently result in even *more* emails because of miscommunication.

It's a never-ending, vicious cycle.

The email from John is just one example of a horrible email, but there are plenty of other examples as well.

The main problem is that most people don't follow the basic rules of good email communication.

I think one reason is a lack of formal training about email best practices. (When was the last time you agreed to the rules of email communication as part of a team?)

Moreover, most books and blog posts about email focus on the *personal productivity and efficiency* aspects of it.

They cover tips such as how to get to "inbox zero" so that you're always up to date, how to batch emails to reduce stress, how to filter them so you're more organized, how to use canned responses to save time, etcetera.

All those tips are great, but they don't focus on a bigger, more essential goal: how to write better emails.

This is what I attempt to cover in this book: simple tactics that will help you write better emails and communicate more effectively with your team.

Why You Should Read This Book

I'll be the first to admit it: There's nothing earth-shattering about the contents of this book.

In fact, many of my tips are common sense that you've probably read somewhere before.

All I did was just consolidate them and present them in a format that gives you simple, actionable steps to communicate better with your team.

I'm guessing you'll probably find at least a couple of tactics that are completely new to you, and that you'll find those enlightening. But even if you don't, the bottom line is this: all of the tactics you'll find here really work.

This book is an excellent one-stop resource that will help you become a much better email communicator.

Here are four reasons why you should read this book.

Reason 1: Email is your biggest time waster

According to a McKinsey study of the average worker in the US, you spend 28% of your workweek reading and responding to email.[1]

[1] Chui, Michael, James Manyika, Jacques Bughin, Richard Dobbs, Charles Roxburgh, Hugo Sarrazin, Geoffrey Sands, and Magdalena Westergren. "The Social Economy: Unlocking Value and Productivity through Social Technologies." *McKinsey & Company.* McKinsey Global Institute, July 2012. Web. 12 June 2014.

If you translate that into workdays, that's all of Monday and nearly half of Tuesday spent on email alone.

By reading this book, you will shave off at least a couple of hours a week spent crafting and responding to emails, which will free you up to do more important things in your life.

Reason 2: Email is not going anywhere

Every once in a while, I read an article that says something like "email will be dead soon" or "no one wants email anymore."

The funny thing is that I've been seeing those articles pop up for the past fifteen years. Their point is that email technology is antiquated and there are better ways to connect and collaborate through social, web, and mobile applications.

According to the *Harvard Business Review*, you shouldn't believe the hype. Email is not dying at all. It's just evolving. It's now "becoming a searchable archive, a manager's accountability source, [and] a document courier." It's not perfect, but it's still a favorite tool among employees for collaboration—even with all the latest social media options out there.[2]

Email might eventually die out, but it's not going away anytime soon. So the skills you'll pick up from this book will serve you well into the long run.

---

[2] Gill, Barry. "E-mail: Not Dead, Evolving" *Harvard Business Review*. Jun 2013: Web. 19 Nov 2015. < https://hbr.org/2013/06/e-mail-not-dead-evolving/ar/1>.

Reason 3: Tactics that are immediately applicable

I'm a big fan of actionable tactics that I can implement immediately.

Those are the types of books I personally like to read. This book is full of such tactics that you can use straightaway with your team members. No high-level theories or strategies. Just simple tactics you can apply today.

I'll also give you examples of why certain things work the way they do so that you understand the underlying reason behind those best practices.

Reason 4: Tips from someone who is married to email

I manage global virtual teams for a living. I'm currently a senior program manager at Cisco Systems (lawyer-required note: the opinions in this book are mine and not those of Cisco) and I work out of my home office in Boston.

The projects I manage are quite complex. Think multi-million-dollar technology projects spanning over months or years. Those projects require an insane amount of collaboration among 100+ team members who live in every major time zone in the world. A huge part of communicating with them is through email.

I also have a direct team of over twenty project managers who report to me about their issues and projects through email.

In short, I'm married to my email inbox to manage my teams, and I get to experience horribly written emails and communication breakdown issues first-hand.

So the tips you're getting in this book are a distilled set of actions that will help you avoid the major issues I've experienced and studied.

These tactics work for me, and they can work for you.

Your Free Bonus

There are two ways to read this book.

The first is to read it for yourself.

The second is to read it for your team.

What I mean by the latter is to share the lessons learned in this book with your team members so that they become great email communicators as well. The value of this book increases dramatically when everyone on a team follows those tactics.

To help you with that, I've put together a couple of files as a free bonus:

1) One-Page Cheat Sheet: A downloadable one-page PDF file that summarizes all the tactics for you on one single page. This will serve as a quick refresher of the concepts and can be shared (or printed out) with your teammates. You can even save it on your desktop as a handy reminder.

2) PowerPoint Presentation: A downloadable PowerPoint presentation with about twenty slides. It also summarizes the tactics, but in a bit more detail than the one-pager. This is a more comprehensive deck where each slide refers to a separate tactic and has a list of high-level bullet points about each tactic's main takeaways.

You can use the PowerPoint presentation during a kickoff meeting with your team to go over the concepts and agree on the rules ahead of time.

Even if you're not going to use all the tactics (or you don't like some of them), you can still use the same PowerPoint file as a starting point and modify it accordingly. This will save you a bit of time in creating your own.

The files are instantly downloadable, and you can share them with your team right away.

To recap, here's the free bonus you'll get:

• A one-page cheat sheet file that quickly summarizes the concepts (in .pdf format)
• A PowerPoint file that summarizes the concepts in more detail (in .ppt format)

Visit the following page to download your free bonus:

http://www.thecouchmanager.com/drabonus

Tactic #1: Assign Tasks in an Email Using the "3Ws"

The "3Ws" (pronounced "three double-yous") stand for: Who, What, and When.

Whenever you assign tasks in an email to someone, those 3Ws are mandatory. If you miss out on any one of them, you'll drastically increase the chance that you'll miscommunicate on what needs to be done.

Here's a description of each W, along with examples to help explain what they mean.

The Who

The first W stands for the Who. This is basically the name of the person who you want to complete a task for you.

When you're assigning tasks in an email, you should start the ask using the name of a *single person*, not a group of people.

That's because if you say something like "All" or "Team," you'll trigger what's called the Bystander Effect,[3] where everyone will assume someone else will pick the task, and no one ever does.

Here are a couple of examples:

---

[3] Darley, John M., and Latané, Bibb. "Bystander intervention in emergencies: Diffusion of Responsibility." *Journal of Personality and Social Psychology* 8.4 (1968): 377–383. Print.

Bad Example: "Team, I need you do this for me."
Good Example: "Sam, I need you to do this for me, and Jim and Karla can help out if necessary."

In the bad example, you're unclear about who needs to work on the action because you're referencing a team instead of an individual.

In the good example, you're directing Sam to take up the task, and asking him to seek the help of Jim and Karla if needed.

Quick side note: There are obviously times when you have to direct a message to the entire team, such as when you need all your team members to take a required training class. That's okay. However, when the task requires only one person to work on it, you want to be very specific about who that person is.

The What

The second W stands for the What. This is a description of the exact task you need someone to do.

Don't be ambiguous and avoid making any assumptions. The idea is to be very clear about what needs to get done.

Bad Example: "Please update the attachment."
Good Example: "Please update slides 4 and 5 of the attached PowerPoint presentation and send me the revised version."

The When

The third W stands for the When. This refers to the exact time and date a task needs to be completed by, which means a specific deadline that you are crystal clear on.

You should *always* use a deadline, even if it's fake, because it gives your recipient both a clear goal and an incentive to get it done.

Bad Example: "I need this in the next few days."
Good Example: "I need this delivered to me by Thursday, July 16, at 1:00 pm US Eastern Standard Time."

Again, every single action that you assign in an email should have the 3Ws spelled out: a clear Who, What, and When.

Tactic #2: Write the Perfect Subject Line

The subject line of your email is like the headline of a newspaper article. The recipient will decide to open your email and read your message based on how well crafted the subject line is. So put in the extra effort to write a well-thought-out one.

A perfect subject line is one that *summarizes* what the email is about. In two seconds, the recipient should get the gist of what you're trying to tell them. Typing "Hey" or "Tomorrow" in the subject doesn't convey anything meaningful.

Another bonus of a well-crafted subject line is that it will help you search through your email archives to easily pick out any emails you're looking for.

Here are three tips to help you out.

Tip 1: Include a summarized version of the 3Ws

If the email includes actions you need someone (or a few people) to do, then as mentioned in tactic 1, add the Who, What, and When, but in an abbreviated way in the subject.

For example: "Chris - need your report by tom COB."

A good habit is to also type [ACTION] at the beginning of the subject line to stress importance.

For example: "[ACTION] John, reminder to send slides

by Thu @ 5 p.m."

Tip 2: Use prefix modifiers

If the email is not an action-oriented one (i.e., the 3Ws don't apply), then add other prefix modifiers such as URGENT, CONFIDENTIAL, IMP (Important) or FYI (For Your Information) in the subject line to explain what the email is about.

Make sure you include the prefix *at the beginning of* the subject line because it might get truncated or missed at the end.

Bad Example: "Info regarding your Dec 1st trip [URGENT]."
Good Example: "[URGENT] Info regarding your Dec 1st trip."

In the bad example, the word URGENT might be truncated at the end of a preview window, especially when viewing the email on a small smartphone screen.

Tip 3: Write the entire email in the subject line

If your email is extremely short, then use the subject line itself as the entire email, just like you would in a text message. Suffix it with EOM, which stands for "end of message."

Here are a couple of examples:

Example 1: "Carol - the team decided on Border Cafe for lunch @1pm <EOM>"

Example 2: "Quick question: did you upgrade to the latest version of iOS? <EOM>"

Tip 4: When replying, change the subject line only if necessary

When you're replying to an email, avoid modifying the subject line unless you absolutely have to. That's because it will make it harder to keep track of the conversation and search for any emails later on.

Moreover, most email programs identify emails based on the subject line text, and some even group them together using conversation threading (where messages are visually grouped with their replies), so changing the subject line will mess that feature up.

So when does it make sense to change the subject line?

Here are a couple of cases.

First, if the topic itself changes, then change the subject line.

It's frustrating and confusing when you start discussing a new topic when the original subject line doesn't apply anymore. Simply start a new email thread with a new subject line and state something like, "Team - I'm moving this conversation to a new email thread so that things don't get confusing."

If you need to include some information from a previous email thread, then copy and paste the text from that email into the new one.

Second, if you're removing recipients from an email

reply due to confidentiality reasons, then it makes sense to add a prefix modifier to your subject such as "[Removing Vendor]" or "[Internal Only]" so that everyone is aware.

In this case, it's technically another email thread anyway because you'll have two separate conversations—one with the vendor included and one without them.

There are of course other situations that require you change the subject line, such as when you're referencing a new ticket or incident number, but the key is to only do it when you absolutely have to.

Tactic #3: TL;DR - Write Emails That are Five Sentences or Less

TL;DR stands for "Too long; didn't read."

The long email syndrome is so bad that now it's got a snazzy acronym response.

If you want your emails to be read, then write shorter ones. According to studies, shorter emails are read more often and are responded to more frequently.[4] (It's not a surprising study, but it's good to know this is backed up by research.)

By writing shorter emails, you'll gain a couple of advantages.

First, you will increase the chances that you'll get faster replies, and second, you'll also *force yourself* to remove all the fluffy language that could dampen the message that you're trying to communicate.

The sweet spot seems to be five sentences or less (there's a whole website about it: *http://five.sentenc.es*), so that's a good guideline to start with.

Also, short does not mean curt. We'll cover how to set expectations with your team about this in tactic 18, so don't worry so much about that.

---

[4] Dabbish Laura A., Robert E. Kraut, Susan Fussell, and Sara Kiesler. "Understanding Email Use: Predicting Action on a Message." *Proceedings of the SIGCHI Conference on Human Factors in Computing Systems* (2005): 691-700. Carnegie Mellon University. Web.

Here are three tips that'll help you write shorter messages that are five sentences or less.

Tip 1: Ask yourself, "What do I want?"

Most people don't know what they want when they send an email; they just think that they do.

This is partly due to a form of cognitive bias called the "curse of knowledge,"[5] where things might be clear in your own head but not translated the right way in text.

If you re-read the last five emails you sent (check your sent email folder), chances are you were not very direct about what you wanted in a couple of them.

The reason for sending an email should be crystal clear, and you should ask yourself, "What do I really want the recipient to do or to know?" as a first step before writing a single word.

Tip 2: Get to the point immediately

After clearly knowing what you want, get to the point as fast as possible right at the beginning of the email.

Don't dance around or pad your message with useless verbiage. Start with the most important information first.

If you want someone to do something, write out the

[5] Camerer, Colin; George Loewenstein; Mark Weber (1989). "The curse of knowledge in economic settings: An experimental analysis". *Journal of Political Economy* 97: 1232–1254. doi:10.1086/261651

actions. If you want to inform them, say so. If you would like feedback, explain that clearly as well.

That's how you keep your emails short.

Tip 3: Highlight if a response or action is not required

If you *don't* need or expect a reply to your email, then state that in your message as well.

At the beginning of such an email I usually type "FYI" or "NNTR," which stand for "for your information" and "no need to reply" respectively. This gives readers permission that their response is not required and makes life a little easier. It also helps them prioritize emails when they're overloaded.

A similar one is "no action needed" where you don't expect your readers to take action and the email is just for awareness.

Highlighting a lack of required action or response helps tremendously in clarifying expectations to your recipients. If you think your readers may ignore an email because no action is needed, then state it's an IMPORTANT FYI.

For example, start your email by saying "Team - this is an IMPORTANT FYI, so please read the note below, but no action is needed from your end at this time."

All those tips apply to forwarding emails as well. So when you forward a 35-email thread to someone, make sure you spell out at the top what you want them to know or do.

To summarize, write short, five-sentences-or-less emails that tell your reader exactly what you want and clearly state if you expect a response.

Tactic #4: Break Long Emails into Two Parts

Whenever you have the option, writing short, five-sentences-or-less emails is *always* better than writing longer ones.

However, in some situations there's an advantage to writing longer emails—for example, if you're summarizing an important discussion with a customer, or you want to highlight the decisions made in an important meeting.

In such cases, a short email could be disadvantageous because you might inadvertently omit important information.

Some people advocate breaking up a long email into *separate email messages*. I'm not a fan of that. When necessary, having one long and detailed "one-stop shop" email where you have all the information for your reader in one place for them to reference is much better than fragmenting the information into multiple messages over time.

The key is understanding *how* to write longer emails so that they're more readable and actionable.

The best way to do so is to break down your email into two parts: a summary section and a detailed section.

Here's what goes into each part.

Part 1: "Quick Summary" subheading

Label the first part of your email with a "Quick Summary" subheading. (Side note: some folks call this summary the TL;DR version, which is counterintuitive based on the acronym definition, but it is commonly used in that fashion.)

This quick summary section should be five sentences or less, so the tips in the previous tactic apply here. It should summarize the main points of your long email and state all actions so that they're not buried in your message.

If there are no actions needed, then state that in this section.

Think of this quick summary section as an executive summary of a lengthy report—an "at a glance" paragraph that gives people the gist of your message if they don't have time to read the whole thing.

The way I think about writing this section is by asking myself, "Have I included all the information my readers absolutely must know if they don't have time to read anything else?"

If the answer is yes, then my mission is accomplished.

Similarly, if you add a large attachment to the email, a good idea would be to highlight the main takeaways from the attachment in the summary.

Don't make your readers dig through a fifty-page Microsoft Word document to extract the one piece of information that's relevant to them. This is particularly important when you email executives.

Part 2: "Details" subheading

The second part of your email should be labeled "Details," "Background," or "Supporting Information."

This is where you write out all the additional information that supports your summary.

Don't shy away from repeating information that was in the quick summary section. In fact, doing so helps reinforce the points again.

The objective of this second section is to add more color or detail to your summary section. Also, if you had actions in the summary, then you could add more information about them here as well.

Here's an example of an email with those two parts.

Team,

I had a meeting with the customer today. Here's what happened.

QUICK SUMMARY

Mike is pleased with our progress. Here are the next steps:

• Christine - please email Mike the proposal by the evening of Tuesday, July 12 at the latest.

• Steve - please set up a meeting with Mike, Christine, you, Michele, and I for the week of July 18 to go over the proposal. You can work with Mike's assistant Sarah to coordinate schedules.

DETAILS

I met with Mike Hernandez, the new VP of business technology services, and discussed the issues we had over the last few weeks. I talked to him about the difficulties we've faced and the challenges we had with the previous product installation. He was very understanding of the fact that those issues were beyond our control, and that we have worked on them to make sure that they get resolved as soon as possible.

He's pleased with the fact that we gave his company the attention it deserves and that we didn't wait for their customer support team to escalate.

Given that he's signed off on the proof of concept, he would like to see a quote for installing the next-generation version for 150 users. I told him that a minimum order would have to be for 300 users, and he was good with that. So we're going to start with 300 for now, and increase capacity in 100-user increments going forward.

For next steps, he would like to see the quote by Wednesday morning. So Christine, please make sure you email him the proposal by the evening of Tuesday July 15th. He also asked me to schedule a meeting with all of us to review the quote and answer any concerns he may have. Steve, when you schedule the meeting, reach out to Sarah first (his assistant). I think Mike mentioned he might be traveling on the 20th during that week and we want to try and get *him on the calendar before then.*

Thanks team!

Notice how the details section adds more information and elaborates on the information presented in the quick summary section to reinforce those points.

Tactic #5: Make Your Emails Scannable

People don't read emails anymore—they just scan them.

If you write emails that are seven paragraphs long without breaking up your text into manageable chunks, your email open rate will go way, way down.

This tactic applies to both your short and long emails. It's about making all your emails easy on the eyes and more scannable for your readers.

Here are a couple of tips to help you out.

Tip 1: Use bullet points for all your actions and questions

Write out every action or question on a separate bullet point in your email messages to make them stand out. Don't bury them in paragraphs because they will be missed.

When you use the 3Ws, every action should be on a separate bullet point for easier readability.

For example:

- **James**: *please send me a draft of the presentation by the end of the day on Monday, Jan 24.*
- **Laura**: *please finalize the report and send it to Donna no later than Wed, Nov 12, 3 p.m. US Central Time.*
- **Susan**: *after you upgrade the server, kindly send the team a note that it was completed by Thu, Aug 3, COB.*

Notice how each of those bullet points is on a separate line and has a corresponding Who, What, and When. This makes it easier for your team members to browse through your email and directly pick their name out from the entire message.

Similarly, type out any questions on separate bullets and lines as well.

For example:

> • *What hotel are we staying at when we're in Miami?*
> • *What charge code should we use?*
> • *Are we renting a car or taking a cab?*

Separating the questions also adds clarity and makes it much faster for your recipient to answer them.

Tip 2: Use subheadings, white space, highlights, and/or bold text

Another way to help your reader scan your emails is to make your words breathe by using subheadings, white space, highlights, and bold text. Don't overdo it though. The point is to make it easier—not harder—on your reader to scan your email for the important information.

Here's how to use them strategically:

Subheadings
In tactic 4, we covered how to break emails into two parts (a "QUICK SUMMARY" and a "DETAILS" section), which are two examples of subheadings you should use when writing long emails.

You could also break up your email into a few more parts like "FINANCIALS," "NEXT STEPS," "BACKGROUND," "ACTIONS," "MEETING ATTENDEES," etc., to make it even faster to scan your message.

White Space

Seeing a lot of words squished together in a single block of text is stressful. Adding white space by breaking long paragraphs into smaller ones, and adding more frequent line spaces between sentences, helps make it easy on the eyes.

Bullets also help in adding white space—especially when you want to give fragmented pieces of information. I don't really know why, but people can relate to bullets a lot better than they do with free-form text, so whenever I get the chance I use them as navigation aids in my messages.

Highlights and/or Bold Text

The final tip to help increase readability is to use highlights or bold text to make your important text stand out.

Highlighting means using the colored highlight formatting tool (I use yellow) to make a phrase or word in your email glow. Both highlighting and bolding work the same way, and the choice depends on your preference.

Some people also like to use ALL CAPS, *italics*, or different sized fonts, and that's also fine. My philosophy is to use whatever means necessary to make sure my important information gets noticed.

There aren't any hard rules about where to use highlights or bolding, so use your best judgment.

Here's what I typically use them for:

• Important dates.
• Names of team members.
• The word "Action."
• Other important information that someone needs to be aware of (e.g., "DO NOT SHARE WITH CUSTOMER").

Again, make sure you use those sparingly. You don't want your email to look like a flashy neon sign.

Summary of the First Five Tactics

The five tactics we just covered are the most important in this entire book. Think of them as your 80/20—your 20% of actions that'll bring about 80% of your results.

If you follow those tactics to the letter, you'll instantly become a master email communicator.

The five tactics complement each other and are not mutually exclusive, so they work closely together.

Here's a summary of those tactics again for clarity. While I'm changing their order so that they're in a step-by-step format, the concepts are exactly the same.

Step 1: Before writing an email, know *exactly* what you *really* want.
Step 2: Write the entire email in the subject line if you can (use <EOM>).
Step 3: If the email needs to be longer, use five sentences or less.
Step 4: If the email needs to be even longer, break it into two parts—a quick summary and a detailed section. The quick summary should still be five sentences or

less.

Step 5: Your subject line should summarize your email.

Step 6: Use the 3Ws (Who, What, When) to highlight any actions.

Step 7: Use "FYI," "NNTR," or "No action needed" to state a lack of required response or action.

Step 8: Make your emails scannable by using bullets, subheadings, bold text and white space.

That's it.

When you consistently follow those tactics, you'll end up building trust with your team that the emails you send out are to the point.

Tactic #6: Show Instead of Tell by Attaching Screenshots

This is my second favorite tactic in the entire book (my first favorite is coming up later).

I love attaching screenshots in my emails for three reasons.

First, they're super-easy to implement. Second, they save me a *ton* of time. Third, my email readers love them because they make their lives easier.

What's surprising to me is that even with all of those advantages, very few people actually use them as much as they should.

If you need to give someone instructions about where to go or what you see, it's always much simpler and ten times faster to take a screenshot of your screen and send that to them instead of typing out a detailed description.

It's a law of nature that people digest visual content much more efficiently than they do text-only content.

The biggest bonus of using a visual screenshot is that you'll reduce any potential miscommunication when you're trying to explain something. So it's a win-win all around.

Here are a few examples of when it makes sense to take screenshots instead of using just plain text:

• To show someone where to go on a website, such as

which tab to click on.
• To give someone step-by-step instructions about a process.
• To highlight a specific slide in an attached PowerPoint deck.
• To show someone an error message to help out in troubleshooting.

To take a screenshot, simply press on the print-screen button (labeled "PrtSc") on your PC keyboard and then paste it into the email directly (it gets saved to your clipboard).

On a Mac, press on "Command+Shift+3" to take a screenshot of your entire screen, or "Command+Shift+4" to take a screenshot of part of your screen. The screenshot will be saved as an image file on your desktop.

There are other screenshot tools that have some additional cool functionality. Evernote and Skitch are a couple of them.

However, my favorite program is called Snipping Tool, which comes free with Microsoft Windows (just search for it in the search bar).

In Snipping Tool, you can select the part of the screen that you want to screenshot, and it automatically snips that for you. The best part is that you can draw an arrow or a circle to point something out on the screenshot using a few annotation tools.

Tactic #7: Spell Out Time Zones, Dates, and Acronyms

"How about tomorrow at 8:30 a.m.?"

That's a typical email note I get from my global team members who want to schedule a meeting with me.

The first question I think about is, "What do they mean by 'tomorrow'?"

If they're in Australia and I'm in the US, and they send the email during my evening, do they mean tomorrow for *them* or tomorrow for *me*?

The second question I ask myself is "8:30 a.m. in what time zone? Theirs or mine?"

Most people naturally default to their own time zone (because they forget they need to convert it), but a few people do the conversion on your behalf and change everything to your own time zone. So that adds even more confusion.

Clarifying what you mean upfront avoids useless back & forth emails.

Tip 1: Get the time zones spelled out clearly

Always mention the exact time zone, day, and date you're referring to.

Bad example: "How about tomorrow at 8:30 a.m.?"
Good example: "How about tomorrow, Friday, July 16,

2016 at 8:30 a.m. US Eastern Time?"

And if it's a sensitive meeting where you want to ensure there's *absolutely no misunderstanding*, it's a good idea to also include both time zones in the same phrase.

In other words, do the conversion for them:

"How about tomorrow, Friday, July 16, 2016 at 8:30 a.m. US Eastern Time (10:30 p.m. Australia AEST time)?"

Use a free website called *http://www.timeanddate.com* to convert those times for you. It's super useful because it factors in Daylight Savings Time in all international countries.

Tip 2: Do the same for acronyms

Similarly, spell out acronyms at least once, especially if you're not 100% sure everyone on an email list knows what they mean.

I once wasted hours of writing useless emails and making contentious calls because I assumed the acronym "PM" in one email meant "*project* manager" when the original sender meant "*product* manager."

Whenever you use an acronym, spell it out at least once at the beginning of your message.

The best practice is to type the phrase with the acronym in parentheses immediately afterward (e.g., "The product manager (PM) is responsible for this task").

Tactic #8: Use "If...then..." Statements

"If...then..." statements are one of the absolute best ways to improve communication flow in your email messages.

Those little gems help in three ways.

First, they reduce the amount of follow-up emails you have to write.

Second, they clarify expectations and assumptions so that there is absolutely no confusion about what could be meant by your recipient.

And third, they hold people accountable for getting back to you by a certain time or date.

Here are some examples of how to use them.

Tip 1: Use "If...then..." for clarity on next steps

"Jennifer - We are leaving today at 3:00 p.m. **If** you cannot be here at that time, **then** please meet us directly at the customer site by 4:00 p.m."

"Michael - You should have all the information you need. **If** you have any other questions, **then** please call the support desk at XXX-XXX-XXXX."

Tip 2: Use "If...then..." to explain assumptions and set expectations

"Daniel, your note wasn't very clear to me. **If** you meant <A>, **then** I suggest we do <X>. Otherwise, **if** you meant <B>, **then** I suggest we do <Y>."

"Kelly - Please lead the meeting today while I'm out. **If** you don't have access to it, **then** please create a new meeting invite and send it to the team."

Tip 3: Use "If...then..." for accountability by your team members

"Sarah - Please let me know whether you want to make any more changes to the document. **If** I don't hear back by Friday Jan 15 at noon Central Time, **then** I'll assume you're good with it and I will send it to the client at that time."

"Jason - Another friendly reminder to get back to me with your approval on the note below. **If** you don't respond by Monday Jun 9 at 9:00 a.m. Eastern, **then** this will be automatically rejected by the system and you will have to re-submit the application again."

Tip 4: Use "If... then..." to have your team members remind you of something

"I'll ask around and get back to you. **If** you don't hear back from me by Friday, **then** please send me a quick reminder early next week so I can follow up on that for you."

"I'm on the road. **If** I don't respond back to you by later tonight, **then** please remind me again tomorrow morning."

Out of all the tips above, the third one is my favorite (using "If... then..." for accountability) because it forces people to get back to your emails, and helps explain what the repercussions are if they don't.

Tactic #9: Present Options Instead of Asking Open-Ended Questions

Email is a horrible medium for brainstorming and long-form discussions.

This is particularly true when a lot of people are copied on an email.

Open-ended questions such as "Thoughts?" or "When do you think we should meet?" invite people to share their never-ending opinions.

So you end up getting a flood of emails with little control over the conversation.

The problem with those types of questions is that they don't provide a structured way for your recipients to respond back to you. So it's a free-for-all.

The best way to ask an open-ended question is to present your readers with options so that they give you a more directed answer.

For example, instead of asking "What do you guys think about this?" you can say "Do you think we should do A, B or C?"

The latter helps guide them on an answer and avoids off-tangent discussions.

Similarly, when you're scheduling a meeting, instead of asking your team "When do you think we should meet?" and getting an avalanche of responses, a better way would be to give them two or three options to choose from.

For example, you can say:

Team,

We can meet for 30 minutes on one of these days:

- *Fri, Jun 3 at 10:00 a.m. US Eastern Time*
- *Tue, Jun 7 at 1:00 p.m. US Eastern Time*
- *Thu, Jun 9 at 7:00 a.m. US Eastern Time*

Which options work best for you?

The idea here is to minimize the number of emails. The more you give options to someone, the greater they'll take advantage of it.

In cases where you absolutely need to ask a brainstorming question, it's best to have a meeting instead of sending an email because the former allows for much more effective dialog.

Tactic #10: Re-Read Your Email Once for a *Content* Check

One of my biggest pet peeves is when someone doesn't read their own email to catch any errors before they hit "send."

I'm not referring to spelling or grammar mistakes. I think folks can be forgiving if you type "farther" instead of "further."

I'm referring to *content* mistakes.

Those are mistakes such as replying to the wrong question, stating the facts incorrectly, adding in the wrong date, or just not making sense whatsoever.

Content mistakes misrepresent what you want to say and usually have the worst consequences.

However, 95% of those mistakes can be easily avoided if you re-read your email *at least once* before you send it.

People sometimes say they're so busy and don't have time to read their emails again.

I get that.

But if you don't have the time to *read* again, when will you have the time to *write* again?

Content errors are the biggest cause of frustration and re-work when it comes to email, so avoiding them is the best way to prevent any headaches.

Here are a couple of tips to help you out.

Tip 1: Re-read your entire email

Re-read your entire email before you click on the send button. Not a portion of it. Not just the actions. All of it.

That's because the curse of knowledge rears its ugly head again if you just glance over specific sections. Your message might be clear in your own mind, but unless you put yourself in your reader's shoes and re-read the whole email from top to bottom, you won't catch those content mistakes.

Some of the things you want to double-check include names, acronyms, time zones, and important dates.

Tip 2: If you're replying to questions, re-read the questions and your answers

This is another form of the curse of knowledge, where you think you answered the question but you most probably didn't. Re-reading the questions as well as the answers helps ensure that you're responses make sense before you reply.

A good practice is to add context in your answers for validation, especially with important information.

For example, instead of replying with just an "Ok," write "Ok, I'm confirmed to meet you on Thu at 10 a.m. Oct 20th." This is not only reassuring, but it gives the other party an extra chance to correct something if *they* made a content error.

Moreover, adding context to your answers is a good habit because if there are multiple questions in that email, and you reply with a quick "Ok," you might be inadvertently agree to everything in that message.

So by forcing yourself to add some clarification, you'll make sure that your answers are not misconstrued.

To summarize, read your entire email, read both the questions and answers, and add validation to your answers for clarity.

Tactic #11: Save Drafts of Repetitive Emails

For the types of emails that you frequently send out to your team members, such as weekly meeting minutes or monthly business updates, it's a great idea to save drafts of those emails so that your team can get used to a specific format.

This of course saves you time and increases your own productivity, but the bigger benefit is that it improves communication with your team members.

That's because you will train them to look for certain areas in the email itself and your messaging will be consistent.

A similar look and feel helps with readability over time.

I have a template for my status calls that I just fill out and send to my team members on a weekly basis. I even keep the same subject line but only modify the date on it. This also makes the emails faster to search for when you or your team want to refer back to them down the line.

Here's an example of my own update every week.

*Subject: Actions & Recording - XX/XX/2016
PMO Weekly Meeting*

Team,

Here are the actions and WebEx recording from

our meeting:

Quick Summary

• **Action (Everyone)**: *Take the Time Entry Mandatory Training by Feb 9, 2016 if you haven't already.*
• **Action (Everyone)**: *The attached compliance report shows a few of you who are non-compliant. If your name appears in the red tab, you need to complete the action listed by Feb 16 at the latest.*
• **Action (Joe)**: *Please reply all to this email (by tomorrow COB) and attach the slide deck that you reviewed on the call today.*

Details

• *Going forward, the business unit product managers will be the main accountable role on all software product issues.*
• *We discussed that project financials is top priority for the team (including forecasting, reporting, and managing expectations with customers) – training sessions will be scheduled soon.*
• *We're canceling next week's meeting due to the holidays.*
• *The meeting on May 22nd will include a new guest speaker who will discuss some best practices about leadership.*

WebEx Meeting Recording
For those of you who couldn't attend the meeting, here's the recording link:
<Link>

Thank you

In the example, I have the main summary at the top, with the actions highlighted, and then all the background information (and recording of the meeting) embedded below.

This way, my team gets used to opening the email with that subject line, and immediately look for the actions listed out in the bullets underneath the quick summary section.

The way you create a draft email is very simple. You just write an email message that you want to use as a template (complete with the right formatting, language, etc.), and save it as a copy in your drafts folder.

When you're ready to send the email, just copy/ paste that email and update it before you send it out.

In Outlook, I have separate folders for my draft emails that are separated out by client or topic (e.g., Drafts for Customer A, Drafts for Customer B, Drafts for Weekly Updates, and Drafts for On-site Customer Logistics), which makes things even more organized for me, and keeps the communication flow consistent across my different teams.

Tactic #12: Write It Now, Send It Later Using Delay Delivery

This is my #1 favorite tactic in the entire book.

Delay Delivery is a feature in Microsoft Outlook that allows you to write an email message now and automatically send it at a later time. You can schedule it to go out anytime from a few minutes to a few weeks later.

Most email programs have this as an existing built-in feature, but some require an additional plug-in.

You can Google "How do I delay sending my emails using <the email program you use>" to learn how to do it using your own tool.

In Outlook, the way you do it is very simple. After you're done drafting your email, go to Options > Delay Delivery, and check the "Do not deliver before" box. Then select a date and time, click on "Close," and hit send. The email will then go to your "Outbox" folder and remain there until the time you specify, when it automatically gets sent out.

You can even go back and change the content of the email (or just delete it altogether) if you change your mind at any time before it's sent out.

There are many ways that Delay Delivery can help you out. Here are a couple of them.

Tip 1: Use delay delivery to send emails when they're most likely to be read

This is about using Delay Delivery strategically so that you ensure a maximum email open rate. According to studies, email gets responded to faster during working hours. This is common sense, but it has actually been proved in an analysis of over two million email users.[6]

If you're typing an email on a Friday afternoon, then it's best to use Delay Delivery to send it out the following Monday morning so that it doesn't get buried over the weekend.

Similarly, if you have some free time to write an email at 11 p.m. on a Wednesday night, then use Delay Delivery to send the email out the next Thursday morning when it has a higher chance it'll be responded to.

This can also be used when you know your recipient is out of the office on vacation so that you send them specific emails when they're back.

Another way to use it is when your team lives in a different time zone. You can send emails to your team when they're awake and active during their working hours.

Tip 2: Use delay delivery as a reminder tool

Delay Delivery is a phenomenal tool to be used as a

[6] Ossola, Alexandra. "Here's What Scientists Learned in the Largest Systematic Study of Email Habits." *Popular Science.* 10 Apr. 2015. Web. 19 Nov. 2015. <http://www.popsci.com/heres-what-scientists-learned-largest-systematic-study-email-habits>

reminder to your team. Here's one example of how to use it.

Let's say your team members need to complete a compliance course and sign off on it by a deadline due in a month. You send them a notification email about that today, and then immediately create two other emails to send using Delay Delivery.

One of the emails can be sent out in two weeks as a reminder, and the other can be sent a few days before the actual deadline. This way you can keep your communication cadence up so your team is compliant, and you don't have to worry about manually setting the reminders yourself.

If you're concerned about the messages not going out (i.e., the technology failing on you), you can CC yourself on all the Delay Delivery emails. This way, you'll rest assured that your recipients actually received the message and also get a nice nudge about it at the same time that they do.

Tactic #13: Don't Reply All (Unless You Absolutely Have To)

When it's misused, reply all is a horrible feature.

It's very frustrating and such a waste of time to have to click through useless back and forth email messages when the topic doesn't really apply to you.

The problem is that because you're copied on those reply all emails, you falsely assume that you have to read the messages and therefore you can't just ignore them.

In my previous job, this was such a major productivity issue that the company literally removed the reply all button and hid it so that employees would think twice about using it.

Here are some tips that you should follow.

Tip 1: Apply the golden rule of reply all

If you're the person replying back, there's one simple golden rule that you need to follow:

Don't use reply all when only the original sender needs to read your message.

That's it.

If you're answering a question, sharing an only-you problem, or responding with a courtesy phrase, then don't reply all. Instead, send your message back to the original sender alone.

Obviously, there are many situations where you should respond back to everyone on a list, such as when you're updating an attachment for your team or sharing an important piece of information with them.

However, most cases don't require that everyone read what you have to say.

Here are some of those never-reply-all statements, particularly when you send emails to large mailing lists:

1. Congrats!
2. Thank you
3. I agree
4. Please remove me from this mailing list
5. LOL
6. +1
7. Please stop replying-all to this thread

Tip 2: Mention when you're removing members from the reply all list

In situations when you want to reply back but only include a *subset* of the original reply all list, you should clearly state whom you're removing and why.

That's because your recipients might not notice what you've done, and you should make them aware of who is reading your response.

Here are a couple of examples of how to do that:

Example 1: "Removing Jim, Steve and Tyler so I don't clog their inbox."

Example 2: "Removing the customer for confidentiality."

Make sure you state that phrase at the beginning of your email so that it's not missed.

Also, if it's a sensitive email thread, you can even modify the subject line with a qualifier such as [REMOVING CLIENT] to make sure your recipients are extra aware of whom the reply is directed at.

Tip 3: Send a follow-up reply all email after any offline discussions

Here's what typically happens in a reply all email chain.

John sends an email to the team. Sarah replies all with her thoughts. Lisa and Chris do the same. Then, a day or so later, John and Chris have an offline discussion about the same topic by talking on the phone and making an important decision about the email's topic.

Neither John nor Chris sends a follow-up email to the thread explaining that they talked and made that decision. This leaves the entire team, including Sarah and Lisa, uninformed about what actually happened.

This is a major cause of frustration and miscommunication among a team, especially when everyone finds out that the subject had been discussed and decided upon.

A best practice is to summarize any offline discussions and *proactively* send a follow-up reply all email to close the loop on a particular topic.

For example, John would send a follow-up message

stating, "Team - Chris and I talked about this on the phone and decided that we will postpone our on-site visit until we hear back from the client. No further action is needed at this time."

Tip 4: State what you want your recipients to do

A good practice is to explicitly state what you want your email recipients to do.

If you *don't* want them to reply all to your message, then simply mention that at the end of your email.

For example: "Please unicast your responses to me and don't reply all."

Conversely, if you *do* want your team to reply all so that everyone is informed of the responses, then type that as well.

For example: "Please reply all to this email because it's an important topic and everyone needs to weigh in on it."

By guiding your recipients on what you expect them to do, you'll reduce the number of misused reply alls within your team.

Tactic #14: Reply to Questions Inline

As mentioned in tactic 5, writing out your questions on separate bullet points and lines helps them stand out to your readers and not get hidden in paragraphs.

To maintain that "easy-on-the-eyes" factor in your replies, it's a great idea to answer those questions inline.

This means answering the questions immediately after the questions themselves instead of answering them all at the top.

Here are a few tips to help you out.

Tip 1: Use a different color font

Make your answers stand out by using a different color font.

Choose a darker colored font (e.g., blue) instead of a lighter one (e.g., yellow) because the latter is harder to see on a white background. This helps distinguish between the question and the answer and improves the readability of your answers.

You can also use bold fonts for your answers if you prefer. The objective is to highlight your responses so that they can be easily picked out.

Side note: If you use different color fonts, make sure your recipients are not color-blind first.

Tip 2: Copy the original questions in your reply

Technically, the term "inline" means replying in the text of the original email that was sent to you (where you typically respond by saying "See my responses inline below"). Although this is sometimes ok, my preference is to copy the entire list of questions from the original email, paste them in your own email message, and then answer them.

That's a better idea for two reasons.

First, you'll keep things "clean," where your reply is not intermingled with their message. And second, when you forward your email thread, or refer to it at a later date, everyone can easily pick out who answered what and when.

Again, the idea is to improve readability.

Tip 3: If the questions were not separated out, then do that yourself

If someone sends you an email with a bunch of questions that are all jumbled together in a paragraph, then separate the questions out for them.

In other words, copy the different questions and list them out in separate bullet points in your reply, then answer them using tips 1 and 2 above.

This makes it faster for you to answer the questions when you see them listed that way. It also forces your reader to look at their own questions and re-read them as well.

Tactic #15: Reply Immediately to Time-Sensitive Emails

When you receive an urgent or time-sensitive email from a team member, it's a good practice to reply immediately after you've read it. This acknowledges that you got their message, and helps calm them down and manage expectations.

For example, let's assume you receive an email stating "I really need this completed within the next three hours," and you can actually get it done. Then instead of just working on the task for the next three hours and then emailing them when you're done, it's better to immediately reply and say that you "Got it and will work on it right away."

That's because most people don't know how to interpret silence and wonder about questions like "Did they get my message? Are they working on it? Did they overlook it? Do they know it's a priority?"

People naturally stress out about things like that and want confirmation that their reader got the message.

Here are a couple of tips about acknowledgments.

Tip 1: Make sure that the acknowledgment is meaningful

Don't reply with just an "Ok" unless it makes sense to do so. If your "Ok" is a quick answer to a question or a simple acknowledgment, then that's totally fine. But when you get an email with four actions and seven questions, then an "Ok" becomes meaningless and misleading.

You should add a little bit more information to explain what your acknowledgment means so that your reader is reassured.

Here are some examples:

• "Ok. I'll get this done by 5 p.m. today."
• "Thanks - I'll reply back to your questions before the deadline."
• "Will do. I'll forward the attachment in the next hour."

In addition, you should also clarify any *differences* in expectations in your acknowledgments so that your reader can manage around those as well.

• "Acknowledged - I will try my best, but no promises."
• "Got it, but I'm traveling and need time until tomorrow afternoon to get back to you."

Tip 2: Spell out your need for an acknowledgment

If you're the one sending a time-sensitive email and you want people to acknowledge that they received it, then spell that out at the end of your email.

Here are a couple of examples.

• "Please confirm that you received this email and that you'll get this done."
• "Kindly let me know that you read this message as soon as you get it."

Again, knowing what you want and guiding your team on what you want them to do is the best tactic for improving communication through email.

Tactic #16: Read the Latest Email on a Thread Before Responding

Most people respond to emails from the "bottom-up" of their inbox. This means that they'll respond to emails in the order in which they were received.

The problem with that approach is that they might be responding to older messages, and the conversation could have moved on with multiple replies to the same subject. In other words, a response could be based on outdated information because some newer messages were left unopened.

This happens quite often (even with seasoned executives), which is another big cause of miscommunication through email.

One reason why this happens is because people batch their emails.

This means that they read and respond to emails in "batches" at certain points during the day as opposed to as soon as they roll in.

For some people, this is by design. They intentionally switch off their email notifications and don't open their inbox until some time has passed to increase their productivity (which I'm a big advocate of, by the way).

For others, they batch because they don't have a choice. They are usually in back-to-back meetings, and can only get to email at certain points during the day.

Whatever the reason, the big disadvantage of batching is

that people don't reply to the latest email on a thread, thereby creating a ton of confusion.

The simple solution is to delay replying until you make sure that you've read all the unopened messages about a specific subject. This way, your reply would be based on the latest information, and you'll save everyone a lot of angst.

Here are a couple of tips to help you out.

Tip 1: Sort your email messages by subject

If your inbox is quite full and you cannot easily spot all the messages about a specific subject, then you can sort your emails by subject line. This makes it quicker to see an email thread because the messages will be stacked on top of each other.

In Outlook, click on the email you want to find, then go to the "Subject" field and sort by subject. All the subsequent replies with that same subject line (including those starting with a "Re:<subject>") will be listed one after the other for you to read and make sure you're replying to the latest message.

Some email programs, like Gmail, have a feature called conversation threading where messages with the same subject line are visually grouped together. So you can also turn that feature on and view all your related emails in one thread as well.

Tip 2: If you make a mistake, correct it by replying back to the team

If you happen to make a mistake and reply to an outdated email, then do everyone a favor and immediately respond with a clarification.

A good practice is to reply all, acknowledge that your previous reply was incorrect (because sometimes your readers don't even realize you replied to an outdated email), and explain what your updated reply is.

For example: "Team - I'm sorry. I just noticed I replied back to an email that was not the latest one on the thread. Based on the most recent information, I agree that we should set up a meeting to discuss."

Tactic #17: Write the Perfect Out-of-Office (OOO) Auto Reply

An out-of-office (OOO) reply is an automated message that your email system sends when you're unreachable through email.

The first rule of an OOO reply is that you should set one up. It's still surprising to me that people either ignore or forget about creating one, which leaves everyone hanging and unsure why you're not responsive.

The second rule of an OOO reply is to write one that's meaningful and contains everything your recipient needs to know while you're away.

There is no excuse to write a sloppy OOO reply such as "Hello - I will be out of the office until Wed," which makes your readers worry about expectations and where they need to go for help.

The best way to show you what the perfect OOO reply looks like is to give you an example of one and break it down for you.

Here it is:

Hello,

I will be out of the office on Thursday, 9 Jan 2016, and will return to work on Monday, 22 Jan 2016. [1]

During this time, I will have very limited access to email (checking it every few days) and have no access to my office phone voice messages. [2]

For questions related to purchasing, please reach out to Maria Davis at (mdv231@gmail.com) or 765-555-2841. For questions related to resourcing, please reach out to Donna Pratts at dprtts@gmail.com or 982-555-2321. [3]

For all other questions or updates, I will read your messages upon my return and will get back to you as soon as I can. [4]

If you need my urgent assistance during this time, you can call me at my cell phone on 913-555-3242 and leave a detailed message with what the issue is, and what number I can call you back on (urgent requests only please). [5]

Thank you!

[1] State the dates: Mention the *exact* dates of when you'll be out and when you'll be returning back to work. Don't just write an ambiguous day like "until next Wednesday."

[2] Explain how you're checking email: Explain whether you're checking your email or not, and how often you're doing so.

Also mention whether you're checking other means of communication like your office phone voice messages.

If you're going to be completely out of pocket, then clearly state something like "I will not have access to my email inbox during this time" instead of saying "I will have very limited access to email."

[3] Highlight who your backups are: Let folks know exactly who your backup resources are based on your readers' specific needs, and include your backups' detailed contact information.

Make sure you have the permission of your backups first before you list them in your OOO.

[4] Set expectations: Explain the expectations regarding responding back to people's emails after you return. This is assumed, but stating it helps manage their expectations.

[5] [OPTIONAL] Explain how you can be reached for emergencies: This is entirely optional, but if you want to let people know how to reach you in case there's an urgent need, then you can list your phone number.

Stressing that it's for urgent requests only usually helps discourage folks from bothering you on your vacation with minor updates.

Alternatively, if you don't want to give them your phone number, you can ask them to email you instead by highlighting urgency in the subject line: "If you need my urgent assistance during this time, please send me an email with the word 'URGENT' in the subject line so that your email stands out in my inbox."

Tactic #18: Share the Rules of Email Ahead of Time

I mentioned in the beginning of the book that there are two main benefits of these email tactics.

The first is that they help *you* become a better email writer and communicator. The second is that they help *your team* gain those same benefits as well, which eventually helps everyone save time and frustration.

To gain the advantage of the latter, you have to share the rules of email ahead of time with your team. This means setting up a short meeting with your team members to go over the best practices you learned in this book.

If everyone agrees on writing shorter emails, better subject lines, clearer questions, and better out-of-office replies, then everyone becomes more efficient at communicating going forward.

As a reminder, I have included a free one-page PDF cheat sheet and a free PowerPoint presentation summary of all the tactics in this book. Those will help make it simpler for you to share those tactics with your fellow team members.

Here's the link again:

http://www.thecouchmanager.com/drabonus

As a side note, you don't have to share every single tactic you learned here. Use what you like, delete what you don't, and add any new ones that apply to your team.

For example, one rule that I typically add is that "Short doesn't mean curt." I let my team know that in some cases, I keep my emails extra-short, which might be construed as rude.

However, I explain upfront that this is because I'm sometimes overloaded with work and I have to get back to people quickly. So I help them understand that if I don't say "please" or "thank you," that doesn't mean I'm being impolite.

Stating that also gives your team permission to be brief and skip out on the niceties as well.

Again, the point of sharing the rules ahead of time is so that your team is in agreement on how you'll communicate, which will minimize any misunderstandings down the road.

Conclusion

We've covered 18 powerful email tactics that help you write better emails and communicate more efficiently with your team.

Here's a quick recap of some of the important concepts.

Tactics 1 to 5 were about assigning tasks using the "3Ws," crafting the perfect subject line, focusing on writing five sentences or less, breaking long messages into two parts, and making your emails scannable.

If you take away a handful of lessons from this entire book, they should be those five tactics. They are your 80/20—the 20% of actions that will produce 80% of your results.

I highly recommend you go back and read them one more time as a refresher.

Other tactics to highlight include:

Tactic 12: Use Delay Delivery to send emails when they're most likely to be read during working hours (my #1 favorite tip).

Tactic 6: Show instead of tell by attaching screenshots (my second favorite tip).

Tactic 8: Use "If...then..." statements for clarity on next steps and to hold your team members accountable.

Tactic 9: Present clear options instead of asking open-ended questions so that you control the conversation.

And finally, a quick reminder of the most important tip of all:

Tactic 13: Don't reply all when only the original sender needs to read your message.

Happy emailing!

Two Quick Notes

Thank you so much for reading the book.

A couple of quick requests.

1) Please review the book on Amazon

If you enjoyed the book, please leave an honest review about it on Amazon. I know you probably get asked this a lot from most authors. However, every single review counts, and it would help me understand how to improve in my future books. Writing a review takes sixty seconds, and if you're unsure of what to write, let me know how one thing in this book has helped you. I read every single review and sincerely appreciate your feedback.

2) Check out my other book: "Influencing Virtual Teams"

If you enjoyed reading *Don't Reply All*, then you'll love my other book, *Influencing Virtual Teams: 17 Tactics That Get Things Done With Your Remote Employees*. It's a #1 Amazon category bestseller about how to manage workers that you don't see. Even if you don't work with a virtual team today, you'll find a lot of the tactics extremely valuable for motivating your own team to get things done.

Thanks again!

Hassan

CPSIA information can be obtained
at www.ICGtesting.com
Printed in the USA
FSHW012133170420
69332FS

9 781532 881138